Pre-Reading Book of Christmas Praise

11 Arrangements for Beginning Pianists
With Optional Teacher/Parent Accompaniments

Gayle Kowalchyk • E. L. Lancaster

Young piano students enjoy playing familiar music. PRE-READING BOOK OF CHRISTMAS PRAISE was designed for those students who have had only a few weeks of study and consequently have limited skills in note reading.

POSITIONS: Melodies for the pieces are divided between the hands. All positions are shown on the page with the pre-reading notation. Some melodies remain within a single position, but others use accidentals that require movement out of the position. These sharps or flats apply to the rest of the measure.

RHYTHM: Students may be unfamiliar with the rhythmic notation of some of the pieces. However, they will usually play the music correctly by memory, or, if not, the rhythms can be quickly learned by rote.

ACCOMPANIMENTS: Each piece in the book has a duet accompaniment. The accompaniments give the pieces richer sounds and can aid the student with rhythmic security. These pieces make excellent student/teacher or student/parent duets. Both solo and accompaniment parts contain measure numbers for easy reference.

Table of Contents

Produced by
Alfred Music
P.O. Box 10003
Van Nuys, CA 91410-0003
alfred.com

ISBN-10: 1-4706-3354-X
ISBN-13: 978-1-4706-3354-7

The Little Drummer Boy

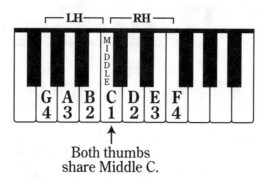

Both thumbs
share Middle C.

Words and Music by
Katherine Davis, Henry Onorati and Harry Simeone
Arr. Kowalchyk/Lancaster

Moderately

Come, they told me, pa - rum pum pum pum,

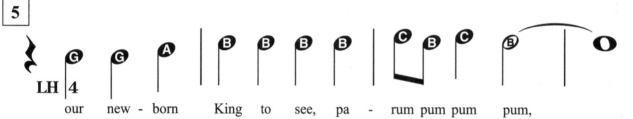

our new-born King to see, pa - rum pum pum pum,

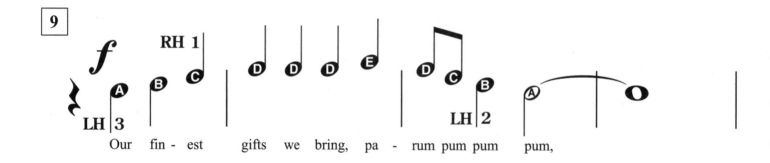

Our fin - est gifts we bring, pa - rum pum pum pum,

Duet Accompaniment: Student plays one octave higher.

3

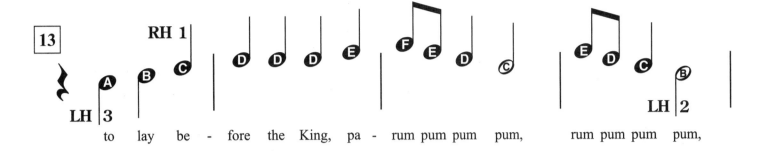

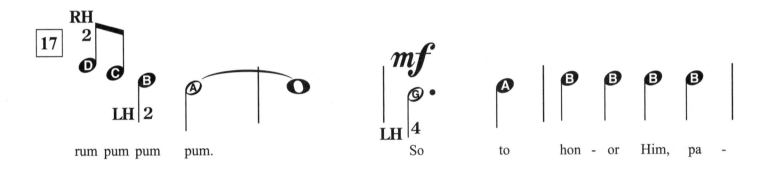

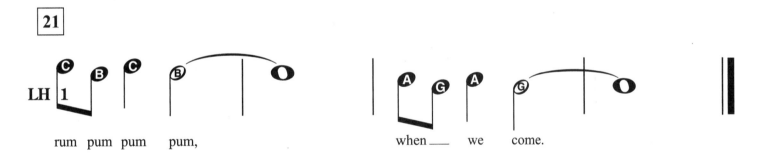

Joy Has Dawned

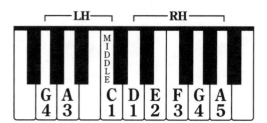

Words and Music by
Keith Getty and Stuart Townend
Arr. Kowalchyk/Lancaster

Simply, with joy

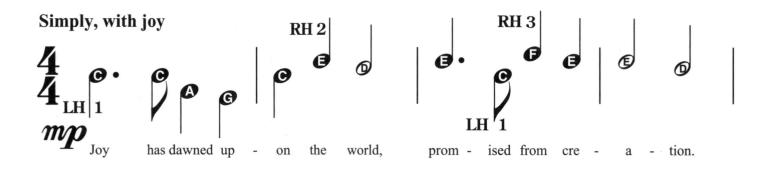

Joy has dawned up - on the world, prom - ised from cre - a - tion.

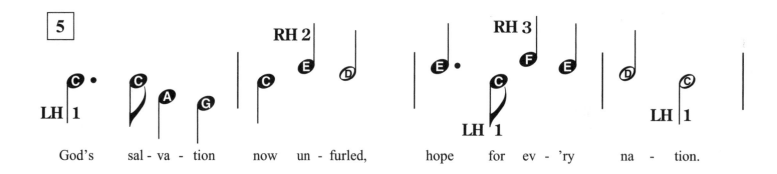

God's sal - va - tion now un - furled, hope for ev - 'ry na - tion.

Duet Accompaniment: Student plays one octave higher.

Simply, with joy

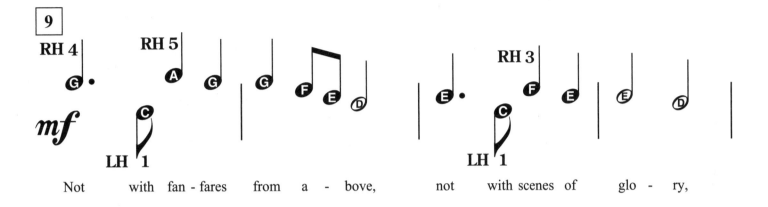

Not with fan-fares from a - bove, not with scenes of glo - ry,

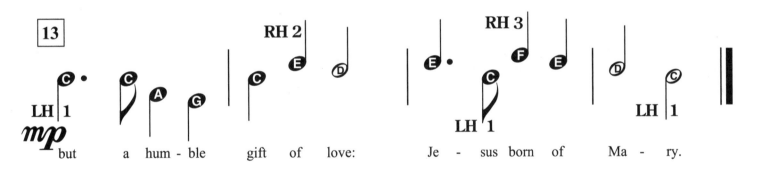

but a hum - ble gift of love: Je - sus born of Ma - ry.

Emmanuel

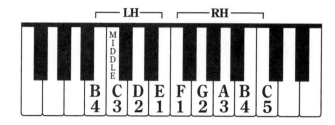

Words and Music by Bob McGee
Arr. Kowalchyk/Lancaster

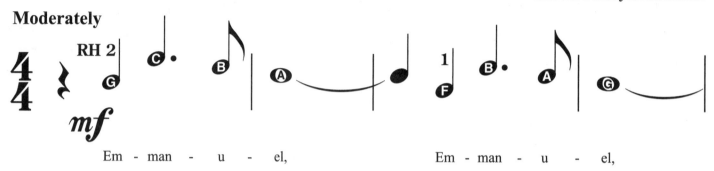

Em - man - u - el, Em - man - u - el,

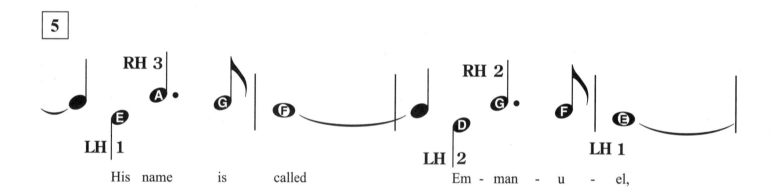

His name is called Em - man - u - el,

Duet Accompaniment: Student plays one octave higher.

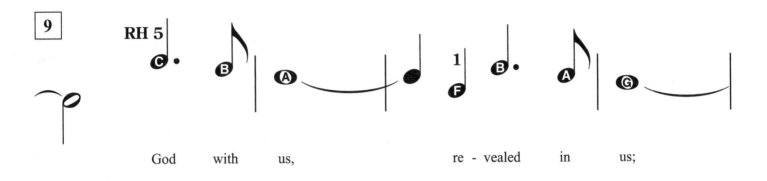

God with us, re - vealed in us;

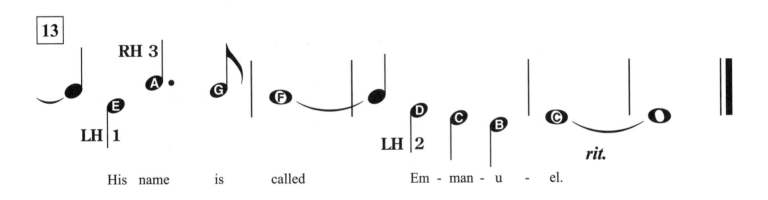

His name is called Em - man - u - el.

Immanuel

(From the Squalor of a
Borrowed Stable)

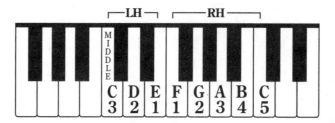

Words and Music by Stuart Townend
Arr. Kowalchyk/Lancaster

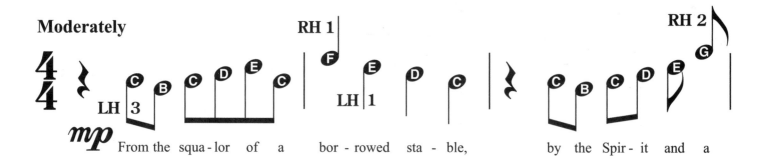

Lyrics: From the squa-lor of a bor-rowed sta-ble, by the Spir-it and a

vir-gin's faith; to the an-guish and the shame of scan-dal came the Sav-ior of the

Duet Accompaniment: Student plays one octave higher.

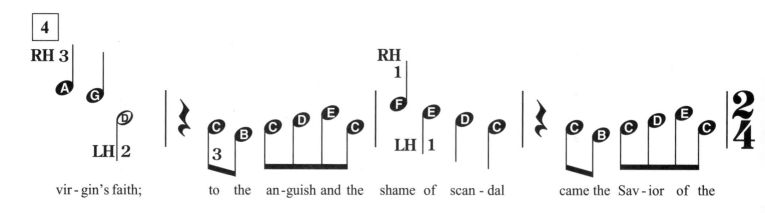

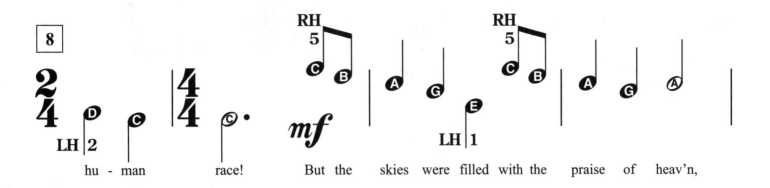

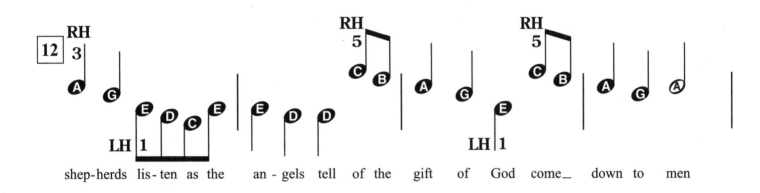

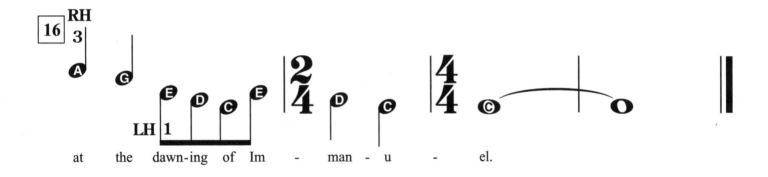

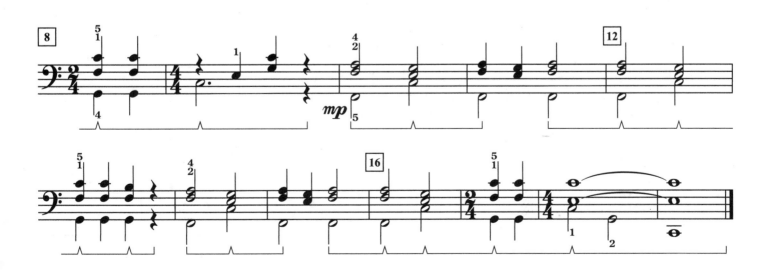

9

How Many Kings

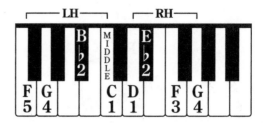

Words and Music by
Marc Martel and Jason Germain
Arr. Kowalchyk/Lancaster

With movement

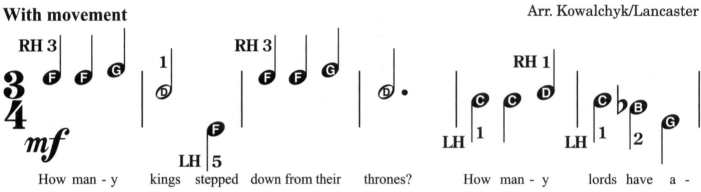

How man - y   kings   stepped down from their   thrones?   How man - y   lords   have a -

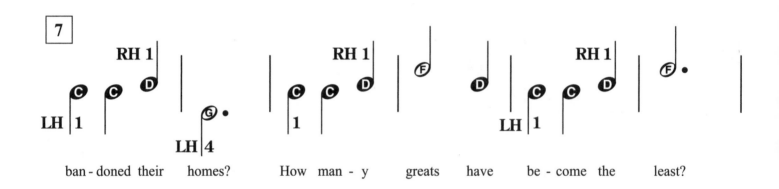

ban - doned their   homes?   How man - y   greats   have   be - come the   least?

Duet Accompaniment: Student plays one octave higher.

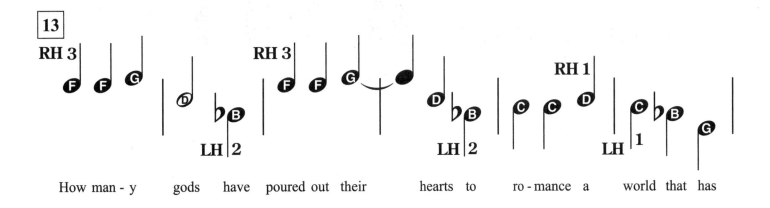

How man - y gods have poured out their hearts to ro - mance a world that has

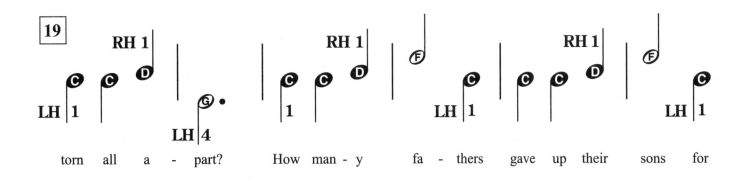

torn all a - part? How man - y fa - thers gave up their sons for

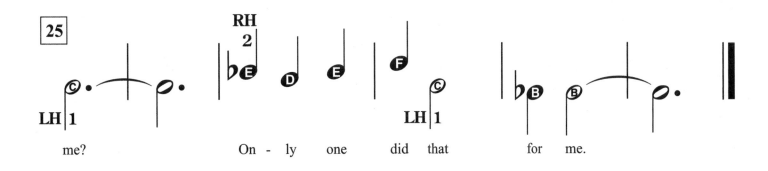

me? On - ly one did that for me.

Mary, Did You Know?

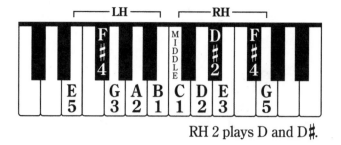

RH 2 plays D and D♯.

Words and Music by
Mark Lowry and Buddy Greene
Arr. Kowalchyk/Lancaster

Moderately

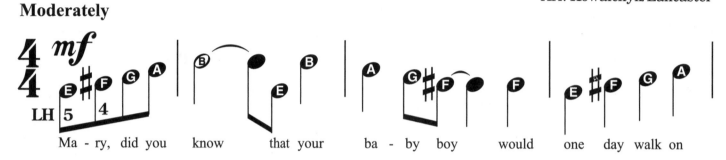

Ma - ry, did you know that your ba - by boy would one day walk on

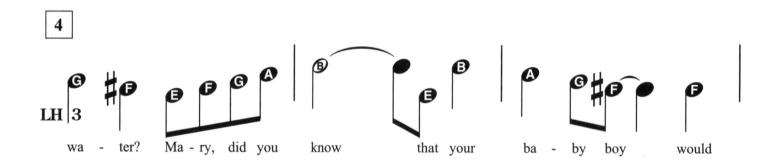

wa - ter? Ma - ry, did you know that your ba - by boy would

Duet Accompaniment: Student plays one octave higher.

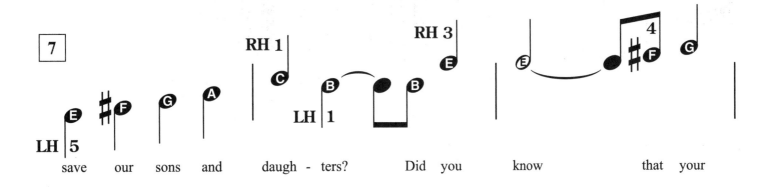

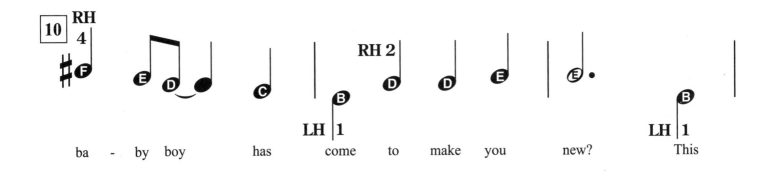

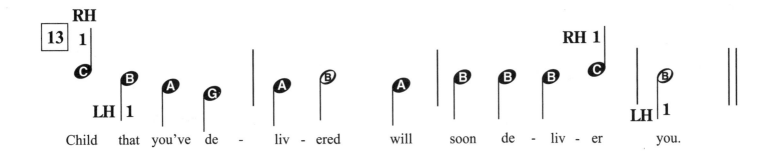

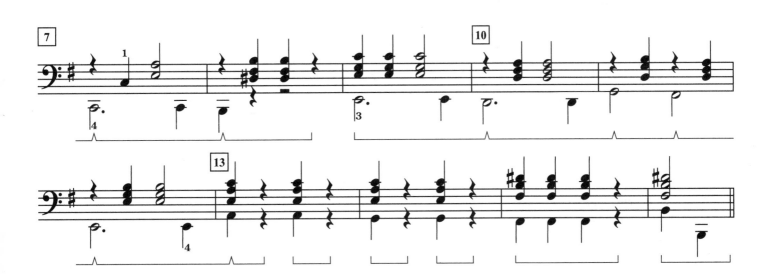

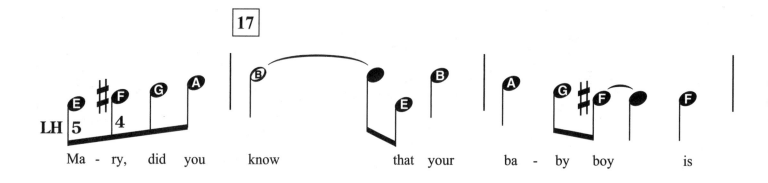

Ma - ry, did you know that your ba - by boy is

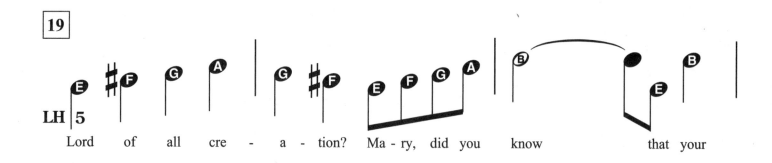

Lord of all cre - a - tion? Ma - ry, did you know that your

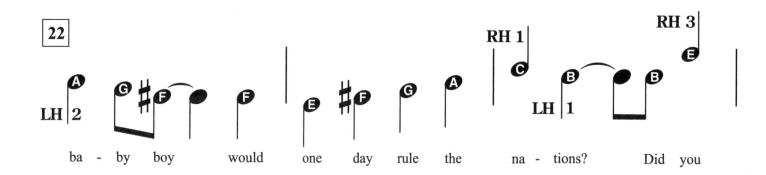

ba - by boy would one day rule the na - tions? Did you

Duet Accompaniment (continued)

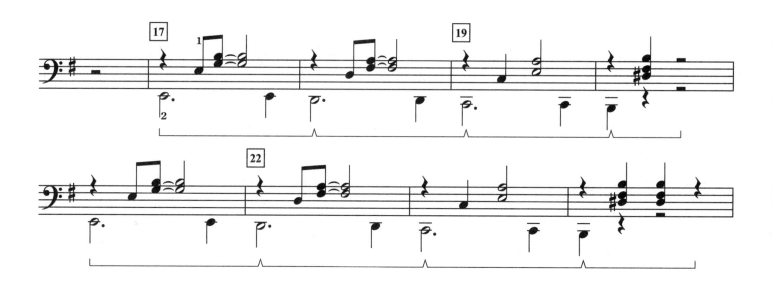

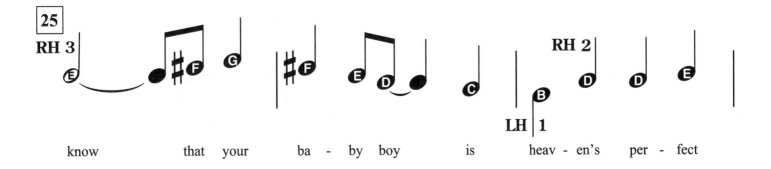

know   that your   ba - by boy   is   heav - en's per - fect

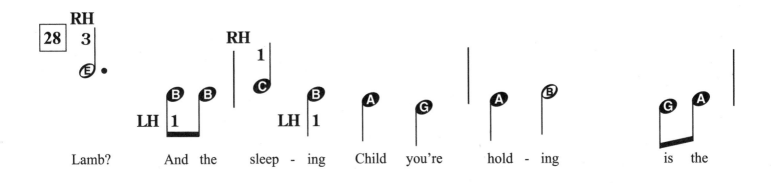

Lamb?   And the sleep - ing Child you're hold - ing   is the

great   I   Am!

All Is Well

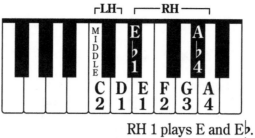

RH 1 plays E and E♭.
RH 4 plays A and A♭.

Words and Music by
Michael W. Smith and Wayne Kirkpatrick
Arr. Kowalchyk/Lancaster

Moderately slow

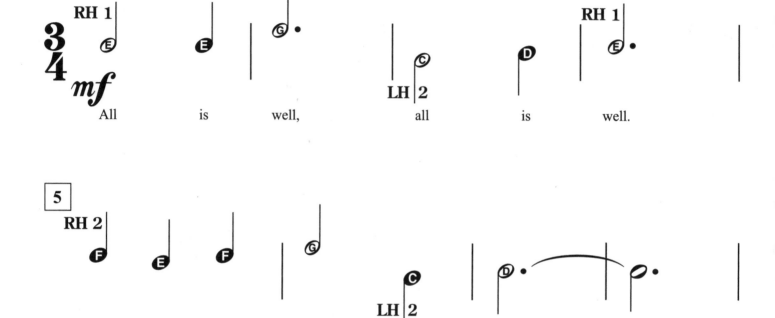

All is well, all is well.

An - gels and man re - joice!

Duet Accompaniment: Student plays one octave higher.

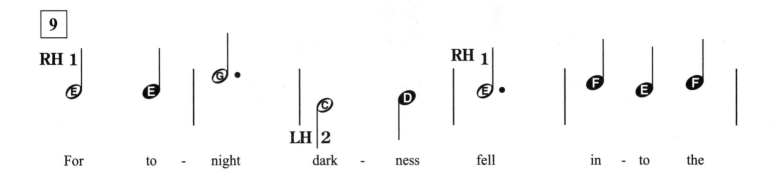

For to - night dark - ness fell in - to the

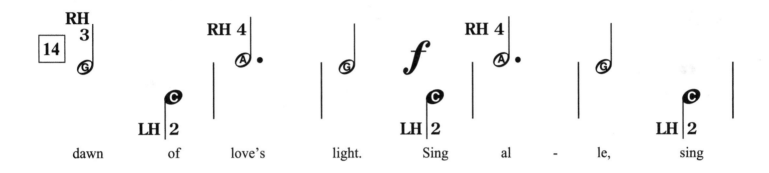

dawn of love's light. Sing al - le, sing

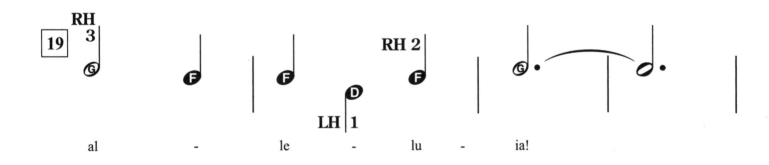

al - le - lu - ia!

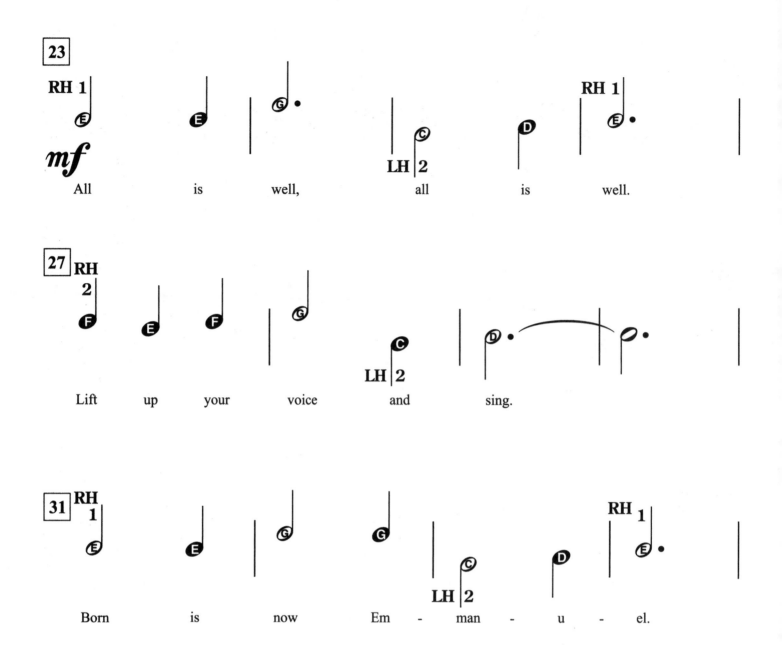

Duet Accompaniment (continued)

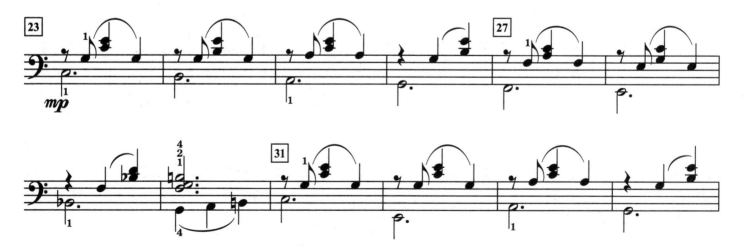

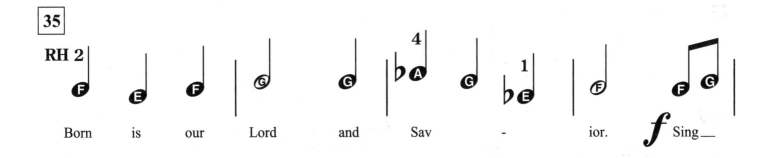

Born is our Lord and Sav - ior. *f* Sing___

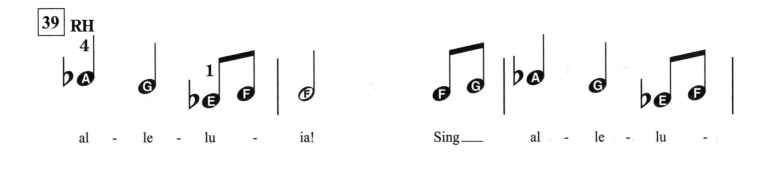

al - le - lu - ia! Sing___ al - le - lu -

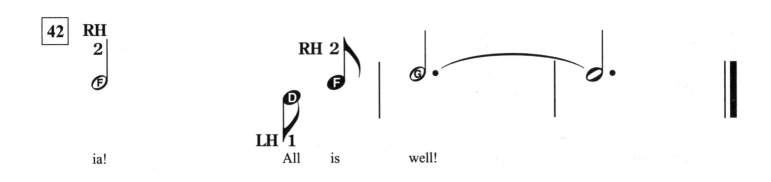

ia! All is well!

Emmanuel

(Hallowed Manger
Ground)

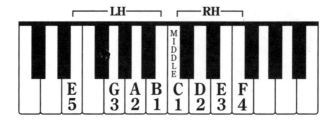

Words and Music by
Ed Cash and Chris Tomlin
Arr. Kowalchyk/Lancaster

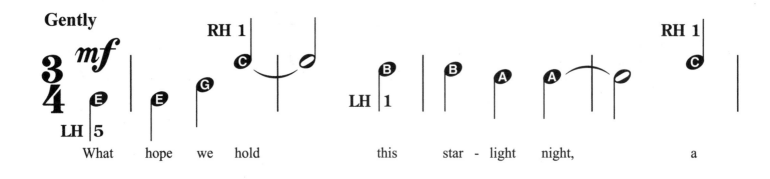

What hope we hold this star - light night, a

King is born in Beth - le - hem. Our

Duet Accompaniment: Student plays one octave higher.

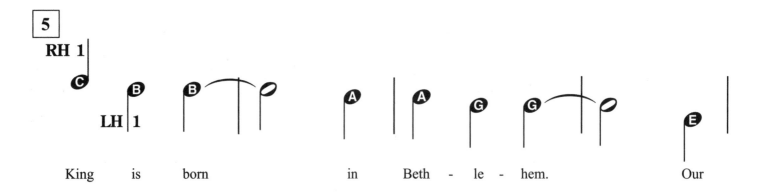

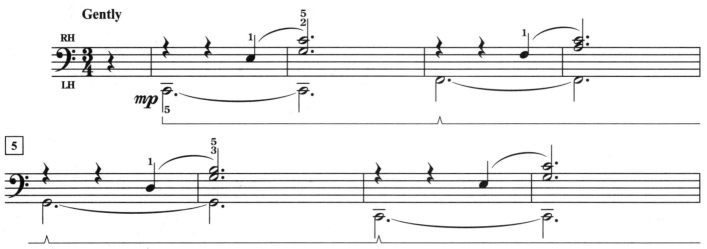

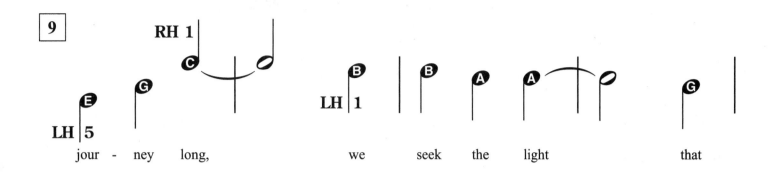

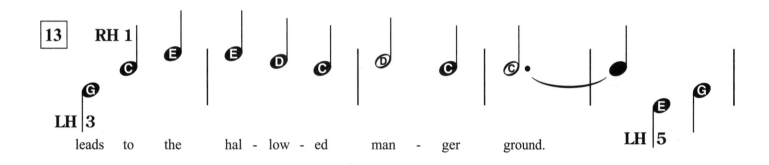

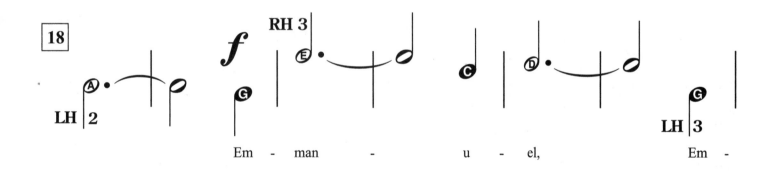

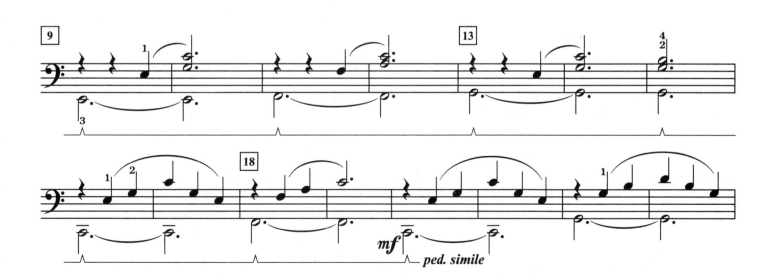

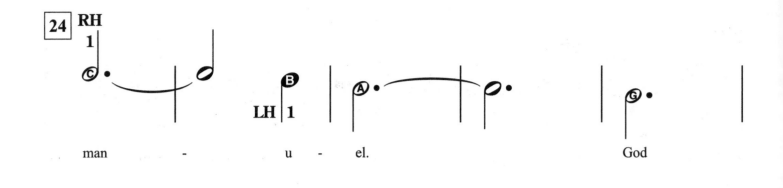

man – u – el. God

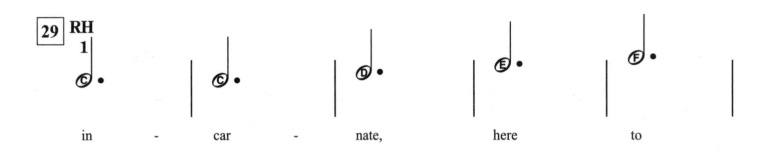

in – car – nate, here to

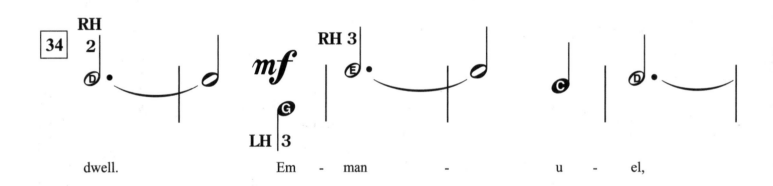

dwell. Em – man – u – el,

Duet Accompaniment (continued)

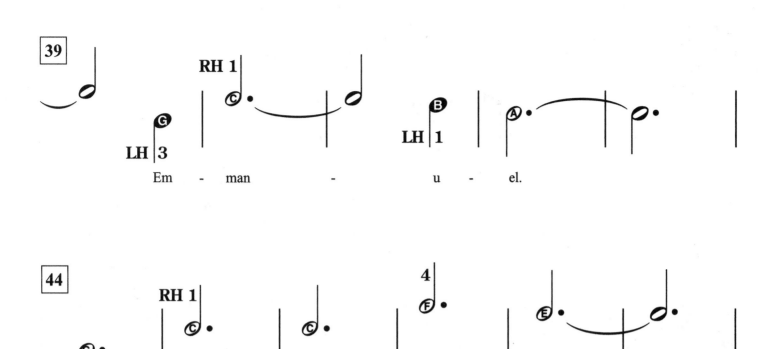

Em - man - u - el.

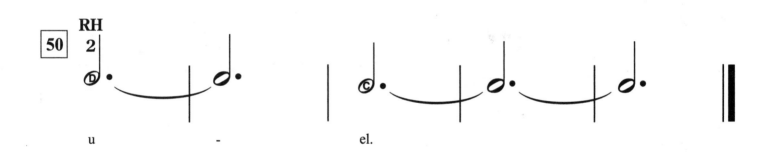

Praise His name, Em - man -

u - el.

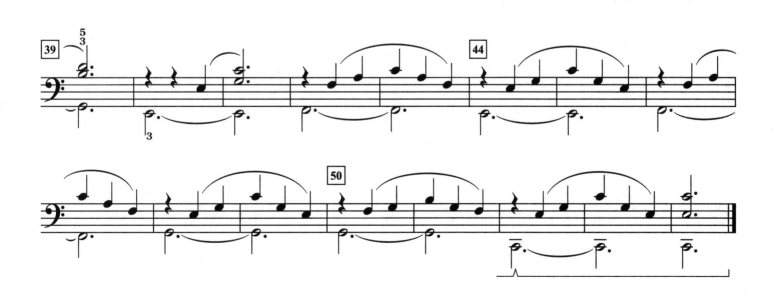

Bethlehem Morning

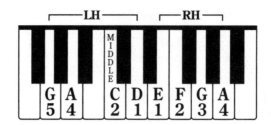

Words and Music by Morris Chapman
Arr. Kowalchyk/Lancaster

Moderately, with expression

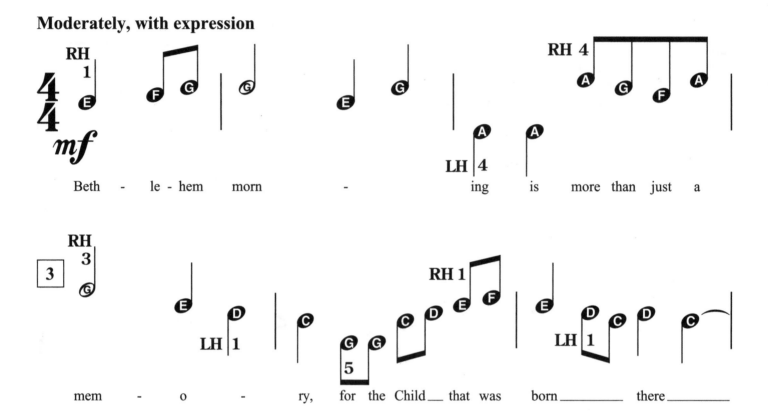

Beth - le - hem morn - ing is more than just a mem - o - ry, for the Child___ that was born_____ there_____

Duet Accompaniment: Student plays one octave higher.

Moderately, with expression

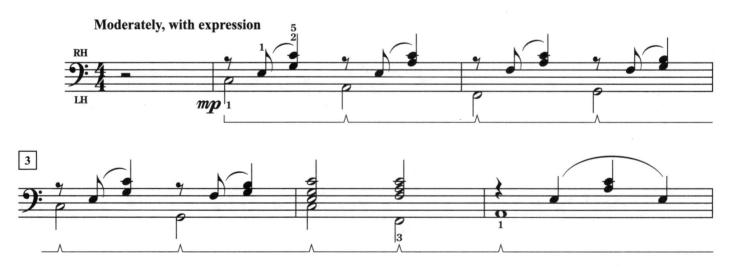

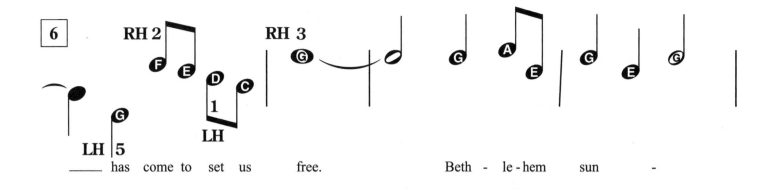

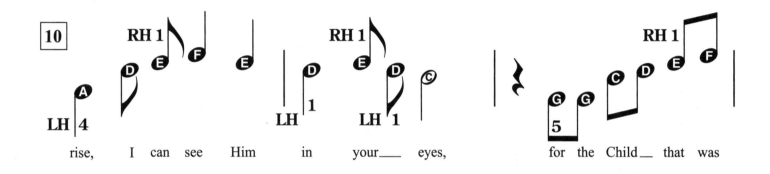

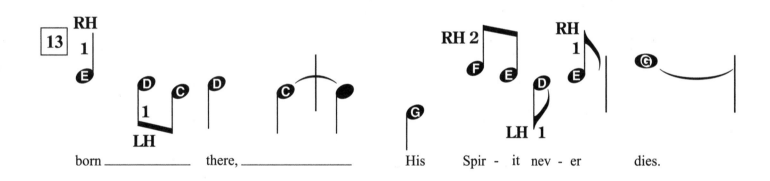

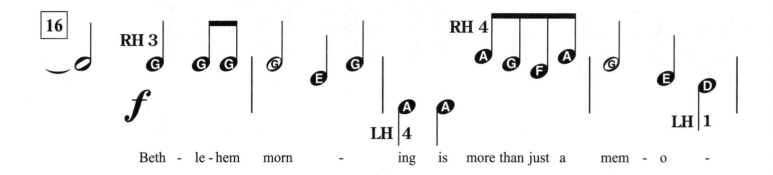

Beth - le - hem morn - ing is more than just a mem - o -

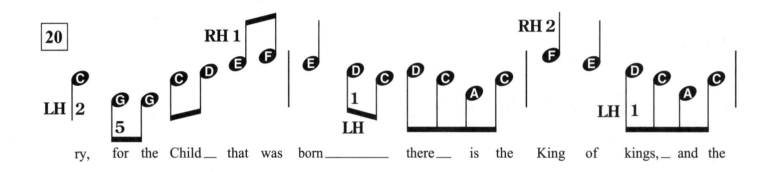

ry, for the Child___ that was born_____ there___ is the King of kings,___ and the

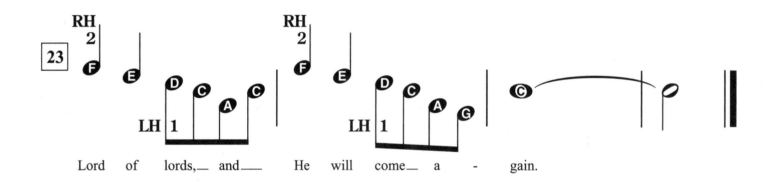

Lord of lords,___ and___ He will come___ a - gain.

Duet Accompaniment (continued)

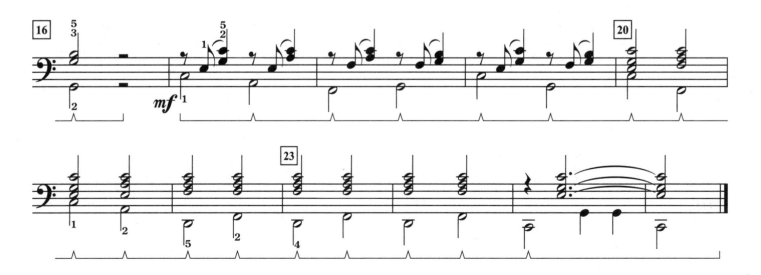

Ukrainian Bell Carol

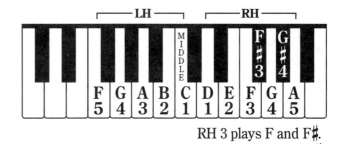

RH 3 plays F and F♯.
RH 4 plays G and G♯.

Composed by Mykola Leontovych
Arr. Kowalchyk/Lancaster

With energy

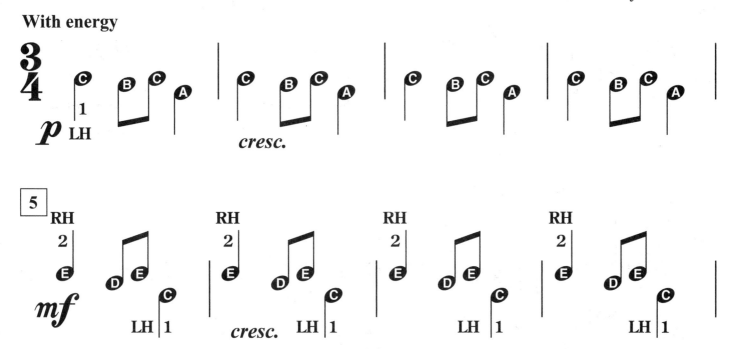

Duet Accompaniment: Student plays one octave higher.

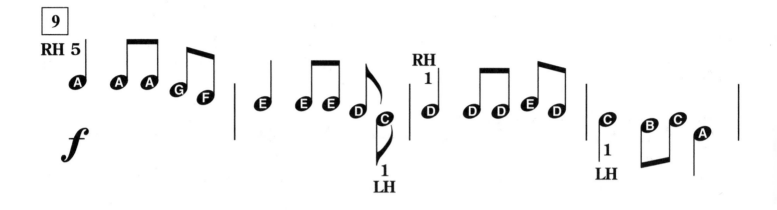

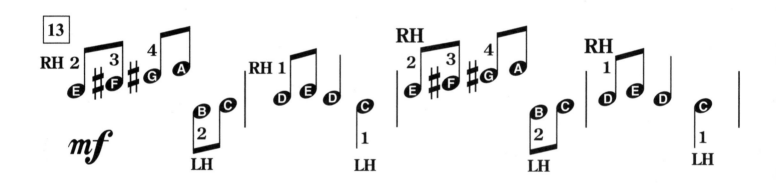

Duet Accompaniment (continued)

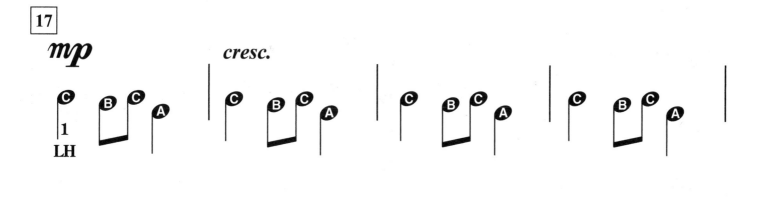

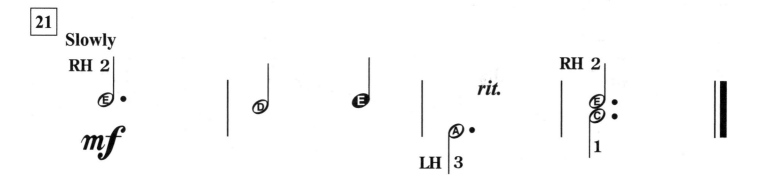

Breath of Heaven

(Mary's Song)

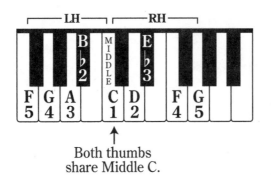

Both thumbs
share Middle C.

Words and Music by
Amy Grant and Chris Eaton
Arr. Kowalchyk/Lancaster

Slowly, with emotion

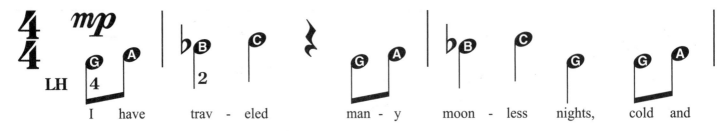

I have trav-eled man-y moon-less nights, cold and

3

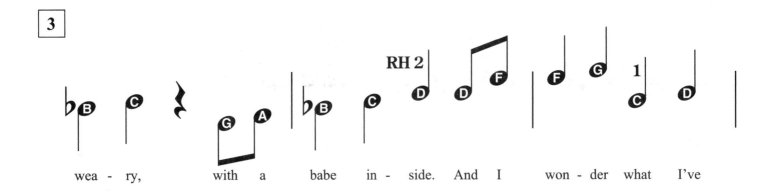

wea-ry, with a babe in-side. And I won-der what I've

Duet Accompaniment: Student plays one octave higher.

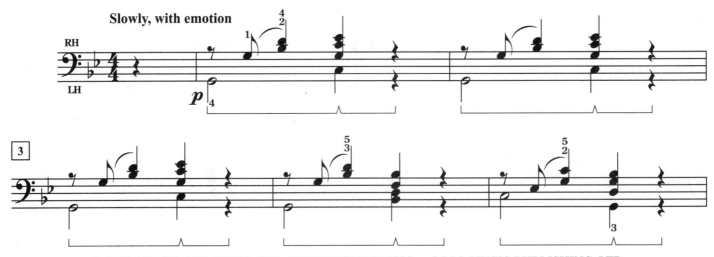

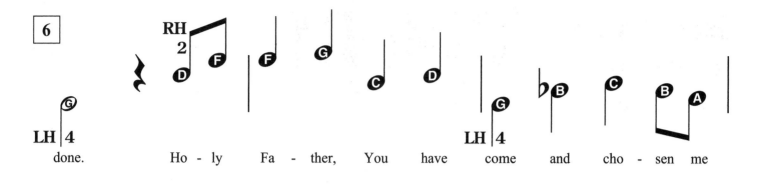

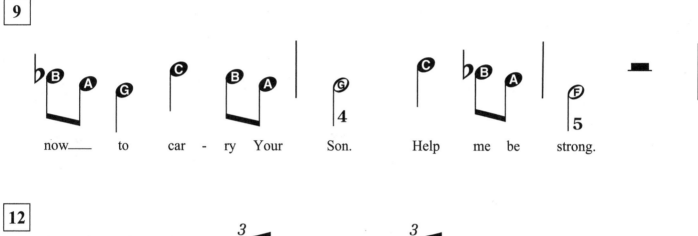

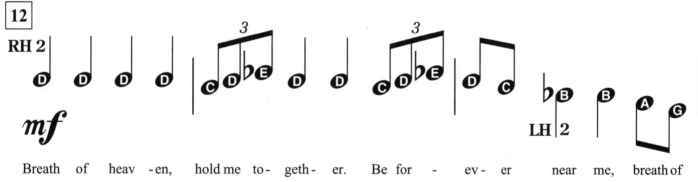

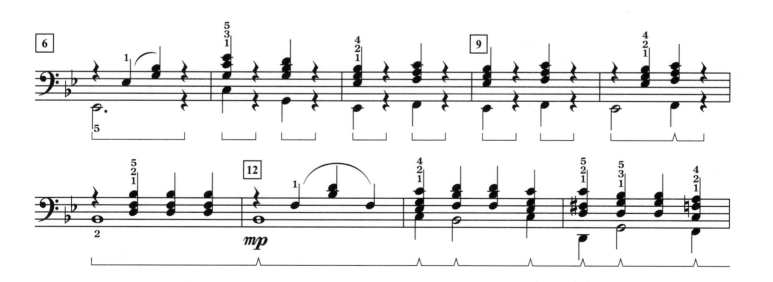

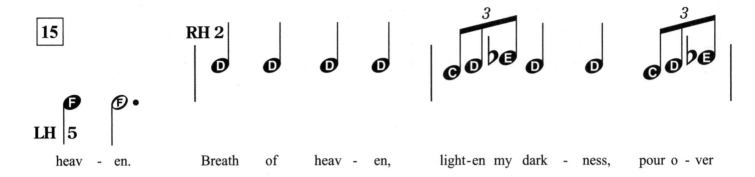

heav - en.   Breath   of   heav - en,   light-en my dark - ness,   pour o - ver

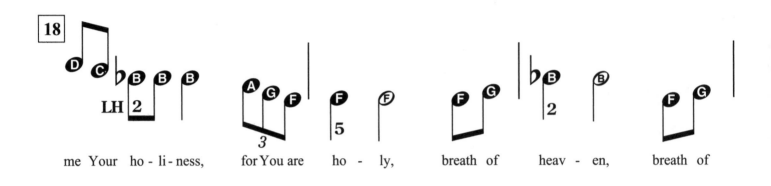

me Your ho - li - ness,   for You are   ho - ly,   breath of   heav - en,   breath of

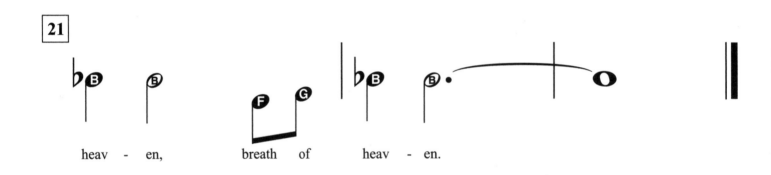

heav - en,   breath of   heav - en.

Duet Accompaniment (continued)

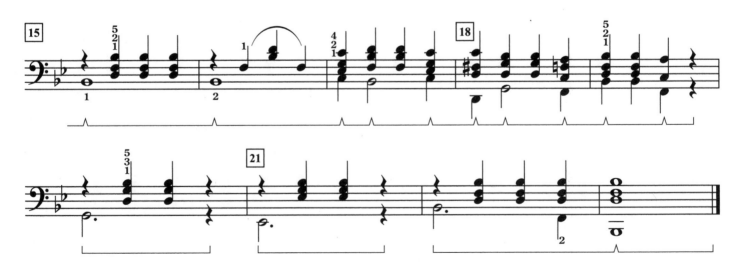